W0017792

CABINET BOOKS, NEW YORK

Inspired by literary precedents such as automatic writing, by the resourcefulness of the *bricoleur* making do with what is at hand, and by the openness toward chance that all artistic production under severe constraint must necessarily incorporate, Cabinet's "24-Hour Book" series invites a number of distinguished authors and artists to be incarcerated in its gallery space to complete a project from start to finish within twenty-four hours.

Written between 10:00 am, 30 July 2016
and 10:00 am, 31 July 2016

When Up and Down Left Town

Matthea Harvey
&
Amy Jean Porter

No. 3 in Cabinet's "24-Hour Book" series

Matthea Harvey is the author of five books of poetry, most recently *If the Tabloids Are True What Are You?* and an erasure, *Of Lamb*, with drawings by Amy Jean Porter. She has also written two books for children.

Amy Jean Porter's drawings and installations have been shown in solo shows in New York, Los Angeles, and Paris, and featured in publications such as *Cabinet*, *McSweeney's*, and *The Awl*. Her books include *Of Lamb*, written by Matthea Harvey.

Matthea Harvey and Amy Jean Porter
at their temporary desks at Cabinet
composing *When Up and Down Left Town*.
Photo taken at 3:44 PM on Saturday, 30 July 2016.

An invisible pair of horizontal zippers holds our world together. The ground is zipped to the bottom of the middle, which is zipped at its top to the sky.

In the days before the Rupture, you rarely looked down (dropped coin, food in the dog dish) and seldom looked up (fireworks, airplane, lost balloon). You shifted your gaze just a few times a day. That's why we went away.

We gently pushed airplanes to the ground where they stayed down. We nudged people up and out of cellars. We squeezed people in skyscrapers down the stairwells like toothpaste from a tube. We ejected trains from tunnels. There were deaths because people panicked, but there are always deaths.

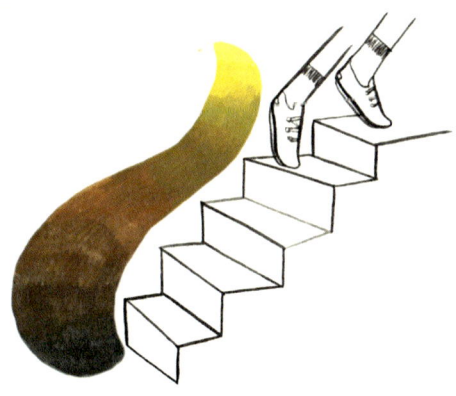

Just two zips and you land-grabbers in your intricate outfits were stranded in the middle. You couldn't see anything below your ankles, you couldn't see anything above your head. (Apologies to the cloud scientist, the pilot, the devoted grower of tubers, the twins who carefully combed the beach every Sunday with matching metal detectors—you didn't deserve this.)

*I watched the last
contrails disappear
from my skies.*

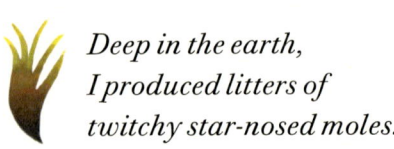

Deep in the earth,
I produced litters of
twitchy star-nosed moles.

You still had each other. You had beds and food. But we took away everything overhead and underfoot. Satellites and stars. All the low-bellied mud-dwelling creatures, though one toad who was on a rock at the time of the Rupture made it through and was promptly put in the Eye-Level Zoo.

Dachshunds, who dwelt almost exclusively at below ottoman-level, were, to all extents and purposes, extinct in Middle, though they thrived in Down, wolfing down each tidbit that dropped from the table.

Some professions immediately became obsolete. With no swinging bars to leap onto, trapeze artists went in droves to actual bars, trailing unseen sequins. Ballerinas shed their toe shoes and slunk away from the stage. The Zamboni went silent.

You didn't panic right away. You were worried, yes, but you muddled along. Frankly, we were surprised to see you frantic gadabouts behaving so calmly.

In those first weeks, you made open-faced sandwiches, tended to your air plants. You pretended we were etceteras, extraneous fluff, a middle-school crush gone bad. You acted as if you didn't know we were gone.

Slowly, slowly I made
diamonds no one dug for.

I crammed the sky
with pink cumulus and
weary cormorants,
who now had fewer
places to land.

The physics are hard to explain. Shall we try? We were still there–you just couldn't see or reach into us. When we unzipped from you, a thin grey membrane of space slipped in between and created a barrier. We instituted the Foot Anomaly because we still wanted you ambulatory. When your foot was in Down you could feel but not see the ground.

It made you walk differently. Some of you strode blindly ahead. Some of you waded as if through caramel. Others tiptoed as if the ground were riddled with traps and land mines. Truthfully, there was a lot to trip over.

Up had no equivalent Head Exemption–if you tried climbing a ladder as if the right rung would give you a view (and now suddenly you developed a love for ladders, who'd been sitting magical and quiet in the basement for years), you'd hit the membrane and bounce right back.

A hawk is perfecting
its parabolas
amongst the firs.

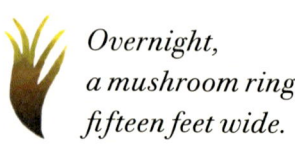
Overnight,
a mushroom ring
fifteen feet wide.

Of course our loss bothered you. How could you not be off-kilter, sloshing through unseen puddles, flinching at the onslaught of sudden snow.

Eventually the inventors sprang into action. There was a run on helium and magnets. But the balloons they sent towards the nothing and nowhere of Up just bobbed at head height and crowded the headspace until they popped. The rabbit ballasted with little lead weights made no burrow into Down. Modified periscopes and telescopes fizzled, failed.

Your lives narrowed. What was the point of travel? The three functional hovercrafts were booked years in advance and if you did manage to get somewhere what would you see? The human-sized slivers of metal at the base of the Eiffel Tower (really more an absence than presence of Eiffel) were nothing to write home about.

You adapted. You carried umbrellas at all times. You threw trash with gleeful abandon into the grey abysses above and below. House-dwellers rigged up mailbox baskets because a letter dropped through the mail slot onto the vestibule floor was a letter lost.

Slowly the Rupture sifted into the language. No one passed tests with flying colors anymore. No one "got down" on the dance floor or sang along to "Get Up" with James Brown. Hand-me-downs became hand-me-sideways. Children weren't grounded, they were side-lined and vertically filed.

Did you think we were never coming back? We were lonely too.

When I say we, I mean Down and Up, but for that year, as you know, we spoke in the singular, the uncomfortable "I."

I made the chandeliers
clang strange
little reminder songs.

*In the depths of the ocean
I somersaulted a piece
of beach glass through
the sand and rocks until
it was an exact silhouette
of Elizabeth Taylor,
age 14.*

We could tell what you missed by what you wrote poems about. Flip-flops and striped socks, water towers and chimney smoke. When we read those, Up felt as if a kite string in the depths of its skies was being pulled; Down felt as if someone was pulling a carrot out of its earth.

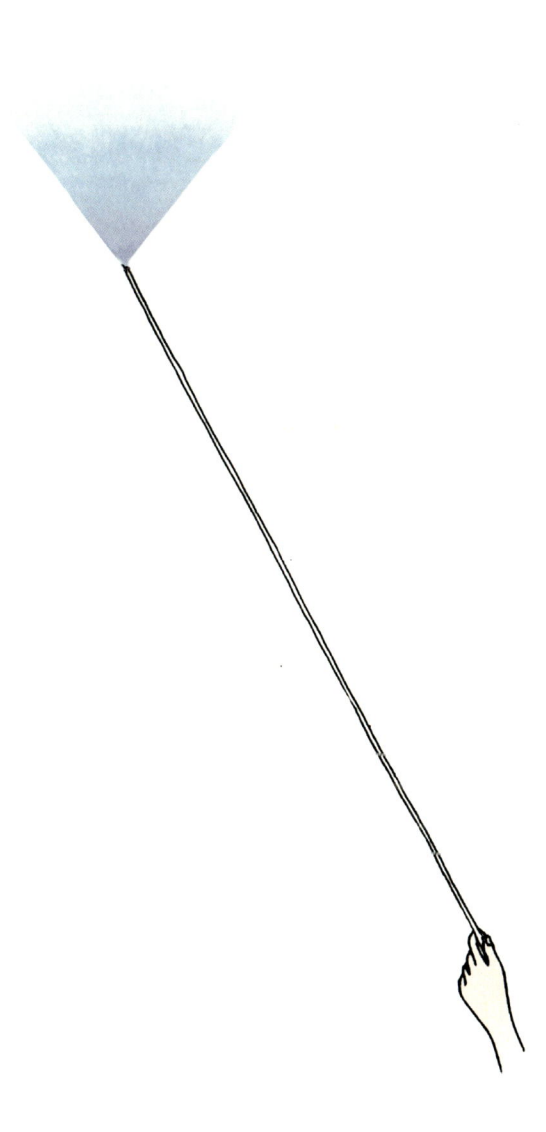

We'd missed things about you too. Up missed dropping fat droplets on your tiny heads, watching a seagull dart down to steal a french fry and disappear into the sky. Down missed skinning your knees on its gravel, watching weeds overwhelm an alleyway.

We zipped ourselves back onto you quietly while you were sleeping. There was a slight shudder, then a settling. We thought you'd celebrate when you woke to see the sun slide up from ground to sky. But you peered shyly out your front doors. You tiptoed down the stairs.

For months you sang songs about sea spray and the acorn mid-fall, as if worshipping the in-between would erase our wounded seams. You kept your rucksacks packed with bottles of bubble solution for Up, cans of spray paint for Middle, and apple seeds for Down.

But now slowly you are coming back to us and us to you. We spy a spade glinting by the door, hear the soft thwap of a kite being unwrapped. Eyes appear at the window. Overnight a zipper of footprints appears on the shore.

FOOD AND DRINK CONSUMED

Saturday, 30 July 2016

10:27 AM black coffee, seltzer (MH)

10:27 AM coffee with soy creamer, seltzer (AJP)

11:40 AM seltzer (MH)

11:40 AM seltzer (AJP)

12:05 PM chocolate chip cookie (MH)

12:05 PM almonds, dark chocolate chunk granola bar, pita chips and hummus, cold coffee (AJP)

12:52 PM Diet Coke (MH)

1:32 PM black coffee (MH)

1:45 PM turkey and apple sandwich (MH)

1:45 PM turkey, brie, and apple sandwich, sparkling lemon beverage (AJP)

3:55 PM clementine (MH)

4:02 PM seltzer (MH)

4:02 PM seltzer (AJP)

4:30 PM caramel ice cream with pretzel cone (MH)

5:30 PM watermelon (AJP)

5:45 PM coffee with milk (MH)

6:00 PM tea (AJP)

6:40 PM cheese puffs, seltzer (MH)

7:10 PM tangerine (MH)

7:10 PM cheese puffs, tangerines, almonds, seltzer (AJP)

7:45 PM cheese puffs (AJP)

8:15 PM Diet Coke, seltzer (MH)

8:45 PM pasta salad, orzo salad, tuna wrap, carrots, cheese, grapes (MH)

FOOD AND DRINK CONSUMED

*8:45 PM pasta salad, orzo salad, tuna wrap,
carrots, cheese, grapes (AJP)
11:15 PM seltzer (MH)
11:15 PM blueberry smoothie (AJP)*

Sunday, 31 July 2016

*7:05 AM banana, seltzer (MH)
7:05 AM blueberry smoothie, banana, seltzer (AJP)
7:20 AM coffee (MH)
7:20 AM coffee (AJP)
8:05 AM almonds (MH)
8:15 AM tangerine, almonds, coffee (AJP)
8:25 AM vanilla blueberry granola bar (MH)*

When Up and Down Left Town
Matthea Harvey & Amy Jean Porter

Design: Everything Studio, with assistance from
Janet Chan
Editor: Sina Najafi

Cabinet Books wishes to thank the Andy Warhol
Foundation for the Visual Arts for its support of this
project.

ISBN: 978-1-932698-77-0

Printed by Bookmobile, Minneapolis, USA.

Published by Cabinet Books
Immaterial Incorporated
181 Wyckoff Street
Brooklyn, NY 11217 USA
<www.cabinetmagazine.org>

Cabinet Books is the book imprint of Immaterial
Incorporated, a non-profit 501(c)3 organization whose
core activity is the publication of *Cabinet* magazine.